DATE		
LaMontagna 11/19/98		

BUILDING WITH CARDBOARD

BUILDING
WITH
CARDBOARD

by John Lidstone

photography by Roger Kerkham

 VAN NOSTRAND REINHOLD COMPANY
New York • Cincinnati • Toronto • London • Melbourne

CONTENTS

Van Nostrand Reinhold Company Regional Offices:
New York Cincinnati Chicago Millbrae Dallas

Van Nostrand Reinhold Company Foreign Offices:
London Toronto Melbourne

Copyright © 1968 by JOHN LIDSTONE
Library of Congress Catalog Card Number 68-54839

Published by VAN NOSTRAND REINHOLD COMPANY
a division of Litton Educational Publishing, Inc.,
450 West 33rd Street, New York, N.Y. 10001.

Published simultaneously in Canada by
Van Nostrand Reinhold Company Ltd.
3 5 7 9 11 13 15 16 14 12 10 8 6 4

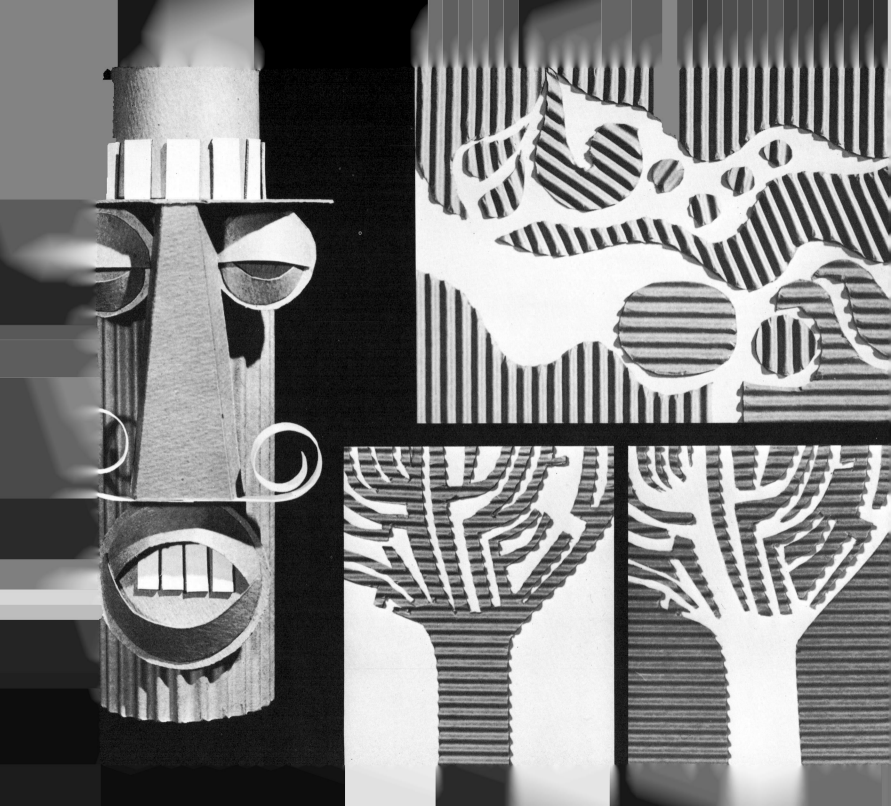

ALL YOURS FROM START TO FINISH

There are hundreds and hundreds of interesting things that can be made out of cardboard, but we are so used to thinking of cardboard in one form or another—boxes, cartons, packing material—as just something to be thrown out, that we overlook its possibilities for creative fun. If you were to take a scout around right now, for example, you would probably be able to find more than enough cardboard—which would ordinarily be discarded—to keep you busy for hours building the most fascinating projects.

You can work with cardboard in two main ways. One is to pick a type of cardboard you like, and let its characteristics suggest what you might make. The other is to decide what you want to make and then find the best kind of cardboard to do the job. On page 6 all the projects are the result of the first method and were suggested by the striped texture and flexibility of corrugated cardboard. Yet, even though they were all made from the same sized sheets, each is very different from the next. All the projects shown below developed out of the second method and have the same theme, a face. While each was made from an identical set of cardboard strips, once again, each is highly individual. Whatever approach you use to working with cardboard you will find the real fun is in originating projects which are 100 percent yours from start to finish.

  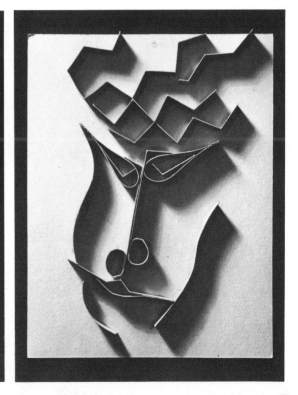

SELECTING YOUR CARDBOARD

When you build with cardboard it is important to find just the right kind for the job you have in mind. If you are going to construct a model house, for example, which must have straight lines, sharp angles, and a sturdy construction, you will need a firm, strong cardboard that comes in flat sheets.

On the other hand, if you are going to make a design that will have twists and turns and curves, you will be better off with a light, flexible cardboard which is easily cut into more complicated shapes or into strips that can be coaxed into exciting design forms.

Choose the sheets or pieces you are going to use very carefully. Make sure flat sheets are really flat. Look out for scuffed surfaces and broken corners. Check for crease marks and faded colors. If you are using scrap material, try to find cardboard that is free of staple marks, gummed tape and, if possible, printing.

Cardboard tubes and cores come in a thousand and one lengths and thicknesses. They will probably give you more ideas about what to build than any of the other cardboard forms. In fact, it is hard not to start using long tubes as pretend telescopes or impromptu musical instruments the moment you pick them up. Cores can, without any alterations, become ready-made bracelets, quoits, wheels, and, in sculpture, eyes and mouths. Tubes make marvelous towers, pillars, legs and arms, and suggest a dozen other uses as soon as you start to work with them.

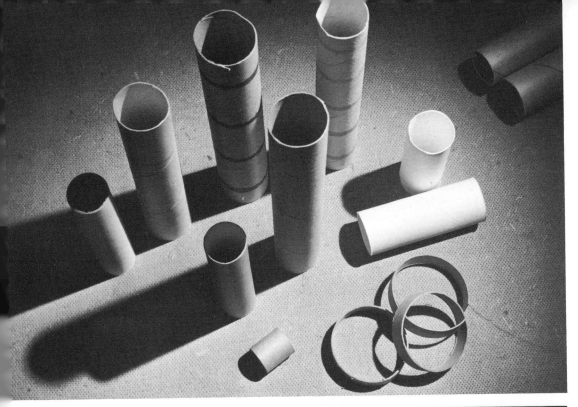

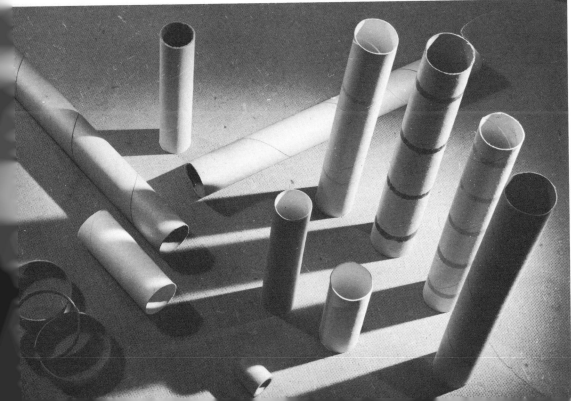

It's fun just to move tubes and cores around to make different arrangements. Look at these four photographs. Each one has exactly the same contents as the next, yet each is quite different. A good project is to collect tubes and cores and, when you have enough, to arrange and rearrange them until you hit on a composition that pleases you. Then you can glue them together on a base to make a piece of cardboard sculpture.

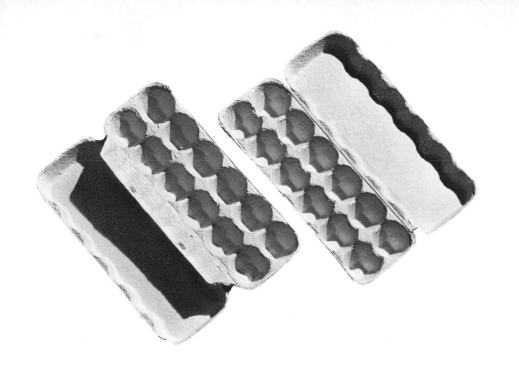

Most types of cardboard are used for packaging. All the different cardboards on these pages are used to package one thing or another. At the left, for instance, is an egg carton made of papier-mâché cardboard which is molded to fit around the eggs it will hold. Below are curved lengths of newsboard which, although stiff, will bend just enough to keep shirt collars neat and trim. On the right, there

are two types of corrugated cardboard; single-faced, above, used to protect delicate objects in shipment and, below, the double-faced kind which is used to make most boxes and cartons. Each cardboard is different from the others because it has a different function. You can take advantage of these differences to find the right kind of cardboard for whatever project it is you decide to build.

Boxes are favorite forms of cardboard because there are so many things that can be done with them. You can hide in boxes, build forts with boxes, slide down hills in boxes; and you can get right inside them and pretend they are cars or buses or airplanes. You can make a variety of things with them—peep shows, castles, modern buildings. A box can be a good starting point for the construction of a tugboat or a truck. You can make a giant piece of sculpture by gluing boxes together to create a super-design bigger than yourself. A box can provide a sturdy base for any kind of cardboard sculpture, or a good frame in which to fit a three-dimensional design. And, besides all this, the tops and sides of boxes can be cut up to provide material for even more cardboard projects.

If you want to saw tubes into lengths which are more practical, use a coping saw or a hack saw whose small teeth will not bite too far into the cardboard. To draw a straight line around a tube, roll a sheet of paper tightly around it so that the top edge of the paper forms a continuous line, and trace along it with a pencil.

TWENTY-TWO WAYS
TO WORK WITH CARDBOARD

Working with cardboard is not complicated. Neither the equipment nor the materials needed are difficult. Certain basic operations are repeated over and over again. Yet you will find that each project needs a slightly different way of working than the last and that, as your ideas become more and more ambitious, you will have to invent your own construction techniques if you want these ideas to become realities.

Very often you will discover that the techniques you have used to build a large and complex model are actually identical to those which were sufficient to produce a fairly simple one. Sometimes an approach that worked well for one model will be just right for another seemingly quite different project. At other times, nothing will seem to be the same and you will have to start from scratch. But, once you get the knack of working with cardboard you will be able to do things with it that you never dreamed possible. Read over these next few pages—they will give you some leads on how to get cardboard to do the things you want it to do so you can build any kind of model or any design you want.

1. Always use a fairly large pair of scissors when cutting cardboard in order to get clean, accurate cuts. Scissors that will cut paper adequately are not always sturdy enough for cardboard.

2. A paper cutter does long cuts best. If you are doing a project at home, perhaps your teacher would cut some of your cardboard with the paper cutter at school.

3. If you are going to fold cardboard, make a shallow cut along the line where it will be folded with a taped razor blade or an X-acto knife. This is called "scoring." Thick cardboard should be "scored" on both sides before folding.

4. When you cut cardboard with a blade of any kind be sure to use a steel ruler or a steel-edged one, rather than a plastic or wooden ruler whose edge can be easily knicked. Don't forget to put something under your work to protect your mother's tabletop!

5.

7.

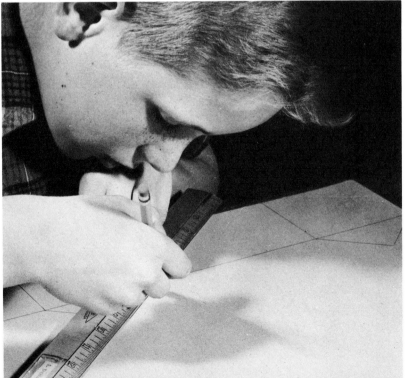

6.

5. Soft shirt cardboard can be scored quite effectively with a scissor blade.

6. In a free-and-easy design it is best to work by eye, but when the parts of a model must fit accurately, each detail should be carefully measured.

7. A scrap of cardboard makes a good ruler when you are trying to measure a part that must have exactly the same dimensions as another.

8.

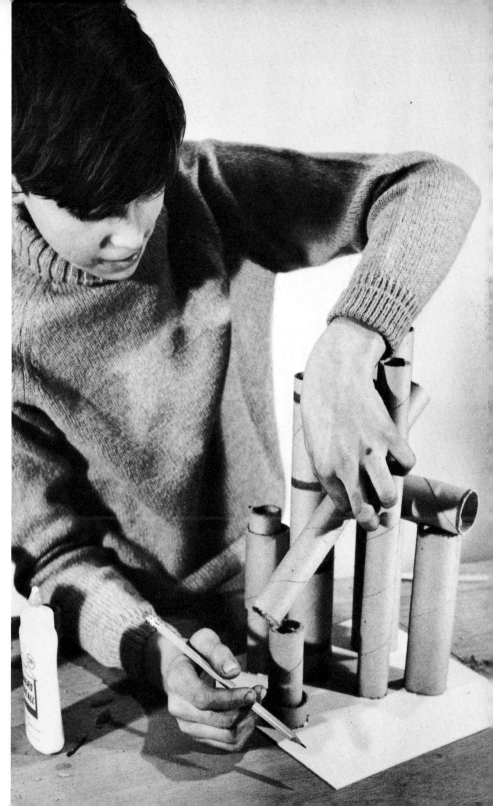

8. When a piece of sculpture or a model is to stand up straight, it must be built so that some parts give support to the uprights.

9. If sculpture is to be architecturally sound each part must help strengthen the next. Peter places a transverse piece across his up-and-down structure not only to add variety to his design but to make it sturdier.

9.

10. If you want to loop a strip of cardboard over itself without breaking the surface, pull it back and forth over the edge of a table to loosen the fibers and make it more flexible.

11. In planning a design or picture it is good to see just how far a certain type of cardboard will bend, so that you will have some idea of the limitations you have to work within.

12. Sometimes working with a tool and your hands at the same time will give you better control of the material.

13.

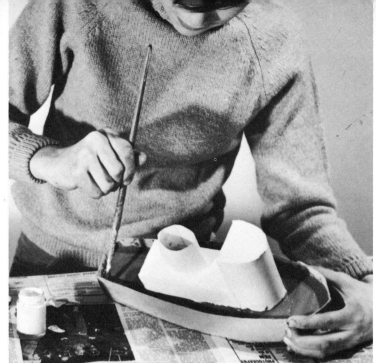

14.

13. A simple, straight-forward color scheme will help the basic shape of your sculpture to stand out clearly, while complicated colors will tend to "camouflage" it and make it difficult to see.

14. Cardboard absorbs water from paint, and can become soggy if the paint is too thin. When the colors dry, the cardboard will warp and the paint surfaces crack. To avoid this problem always use thick poster paint to decorate your models.

15. Cardboard models kept free of excess glue always look clean and trim. Wet glue can be easily wiped off with a piece of paper toweling or a clean cloth, or scraped off with a scrap of cardboard.

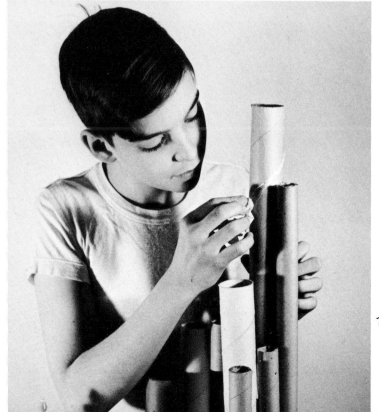

15.

16, 17: Squeezing a supply of quick-drying glue on a square of cardboard or paper and applying it with a length of scrap cardboard will help you do a neat and accurate job of gluing.

18. Paper clips will help to keep the pieces of your model in place while the glue dries.

19, 20: Staples and sticky tape can often take the place of glue.

21. Units to be used can be made up ahead of time so the glued surfaces can dry while you work on the model itself.

22. If you want a piece that is extended out from your model to dry in position, you must support it so that it will not droop while the glue that will eventually hold it in place dries.

16.

18.

17.

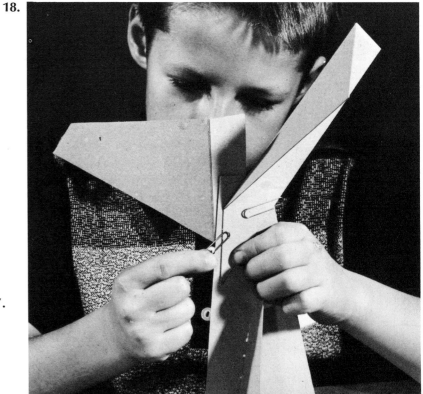

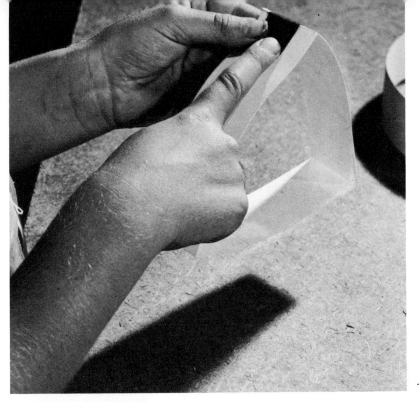

20.

19.

22.

21.

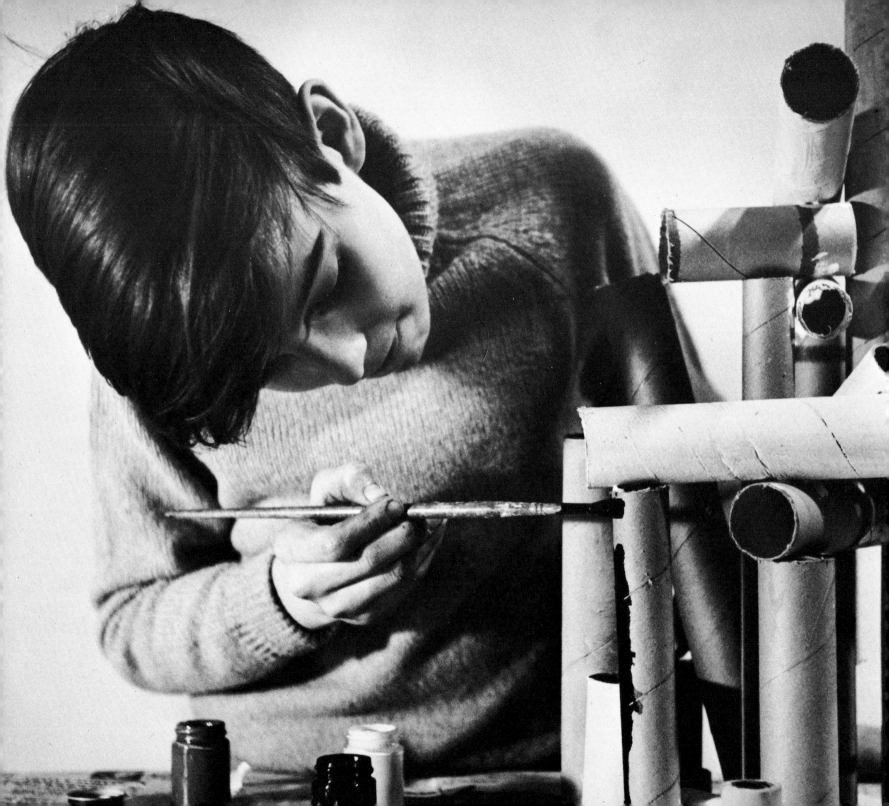

EXPLOSION
IN A TELESCOPE FACTORY

Cardboard sculpture always reflects the character of the cardboard from which it is made. Peter's sculpture is made from cardboard tubes and cores and so, like a pipe organ, is dominated by long, cylindrical shapes. His title for it, "Explosion in a Telescope Factory," indicates the sort of feeling we get when we look at it. The best cardboard sculpture makes use of the special type of cardboard from which it is constructed, emphasizing its characteristics rather than disguising them.

When you work on a piece of sculpture as large as Peter's, gluing one piece of cardboard to the next can become quite exciting. Just trying to get it to stand up straight is a challenge. Eventually, when things are going well, you begin to take a few chances—balancing one tube on another in an unlikely position; placing another where it will look just right, but where there is only a fraction of an inch of surface on which to apply glue. Once you get involved in sculpture, time flies and, before you know it, you will have used up what looked to be a long evening. You are apt to find yourself trying to convince your parents that your project is terribly important and you should be allowed to stay up the extra half hour you need to apply the finishing touches. Your sculpture will turn out best if you remember it is three-dimensional, and that it will be viewed from all sides and even from above. Remembering this, you should keep studying it from all angles so that your composition will not have a front or back, but will be equally effective from all positions.

Peter has made a collection of cardboard tubes to provide the material for a piece of sculpture. He uses a coping saw to cut the tubes into a variety of interesting lengths. So that it will stand up straight when it is glued to its base, and so one tube can be easily glued to the next, he is careful to make each of his cuts at a correct angle to the length of the tube.

Peter uses a flat square of cardboard for the base of his sculpture. He decides what lengths he will use for his uprights and carefully marks where each will be placed.

He puts a ring of glue where each will stand.

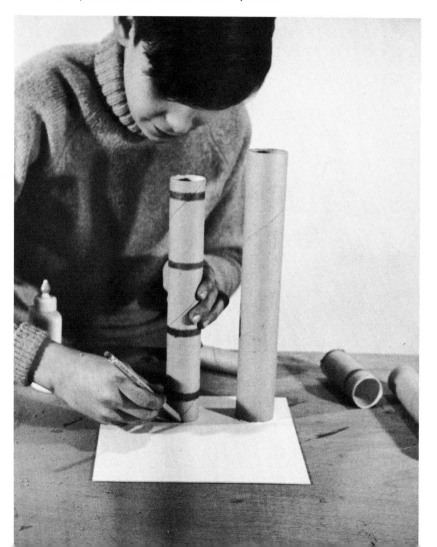

He positions each tube so that the edge of its circular end
settles into the glue. Because Peter was careful to saw at right
angles across each tube he has little difficulty in getting his
uprights to stand straight.

He adds a horizontal tube, and his composition begins to take
on new excitement.

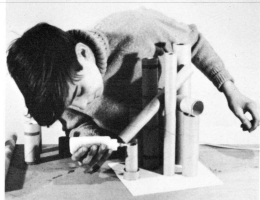

Peter adds a fresh note to his sculpture by gluing small tubes inside larger ones. He breaks the left-right up-down pattern by including a diagonal, and stretches out his composition by topping it off with an especially long vertical tube. Now that the sculpture is well under way, he positions tubes at odd angles to add life to his design.

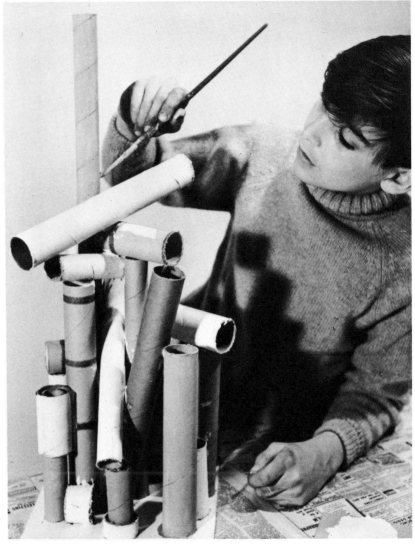

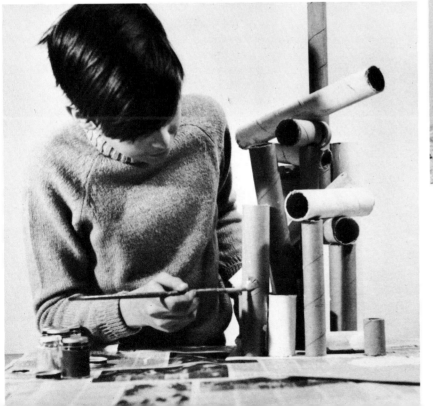

Satisfied that his sculpture is structurally complete, Peter uses poster paint to make his composition even more effective.

29

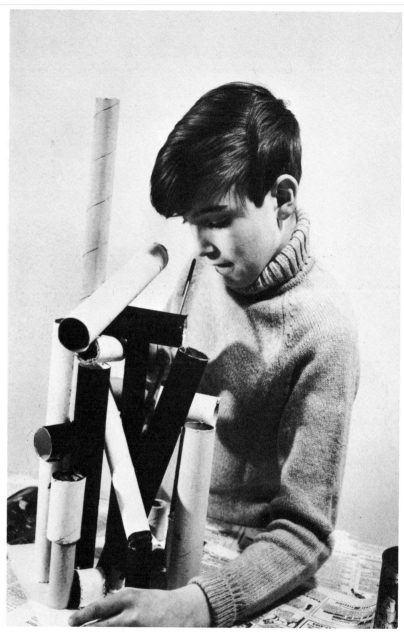

Cardboard tubes are made in a special way so that they will be straight, rigid, strong, and hollow. In his second sculpture Peter takes advantage of these characteristics. He doesn't try to bend the tubes because he knows they would buckle, and he doesn't try to cut them into shapes because it is obvious that it would be difficult to make any kind of cut more complicated than a straight line. As a result, Peter experienced no difficulties in putting his construction together, and ended up with a handsome and sturdy piece of sculpture.

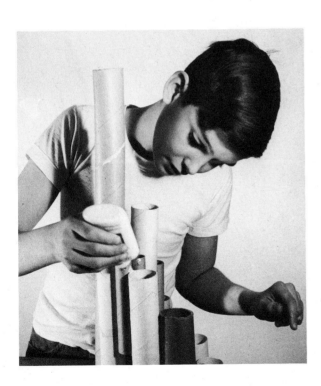

Wing (Make one)

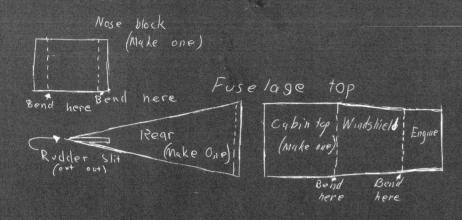

Nose block (Make one)

Bend here   Bend here

Fuselage top

Rudder Slit (cut out)

Rear (Make One)

Cabin top (Make one) | Windshield | Engine

Bend here   Bend here

Fuselage Bottom (Make One)

Wheels (make two)

Wheel struts and axle (make one)

(Bend into a Square "U")

Bend here   Bend here

Wing Struts (make two)

Rudder (make one)

Elevator (Make one)

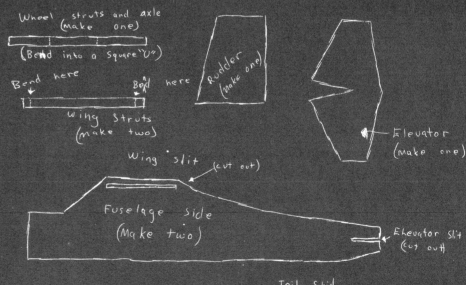

Peter Kelley

Wing slit (cut out)

Fuselage Side (Make two)

Elevator Slit (cut out)

Tail skid (make one)

Bend here

PETER BUILDS A PLANE

Just like a professional aeronautical designer, Peter had to take into account the qualities of the material with which he was going to work when he designed his plane. If you look at his plans you will see that he has avoided a cylindrical shape and chosen to work with a fuselage whose four panels come together in a square engine block at the nose and a point at the tail. Although he could have successfully completed a rounded body in balsa wood which he could carve and sand to shape, he would have run into trouble trying to squeeze and push flat sheets of cardboard into a sleek, streamlined form. Most of the time you can work out cardboard designs with the cardboard itself, but, in this case of a realistic, complicated model such as Peter's, it is better to sketch out preliminary plans as he has done here.

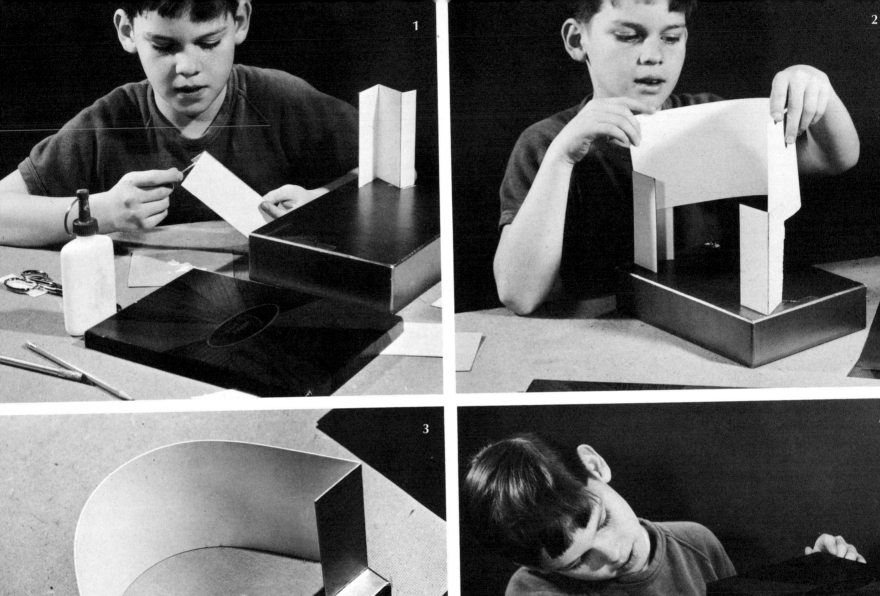

A MINIATURE STAGE
FROM A CARDBOARD BOX

Neil likes to build models of real things. Here we see him making a miniature stage from a cardboard box. He turns the bottom of the box upside down and glues two zigzags of cardboard (**1**) to its front corners. The zigzags hide the wings of the stage and provide "keys" into which the background can fit. See how a piece of paper cut the height of the stage can be slipped into the "keys" (**2**), and sprung to form an arc at the back of the stage (**3**). Neil completes his model by setting the lid of the box on top (**4**). When he wants to change the setting, he takes off the lid and puts a different length of paper into the "keys" (**5**). He then studies the new arrangement wondering if it is what he wants for the scene he has in mind (**6**).

It is fun to build a miniature stage, but it is just as much fun to play with it after you have finished it.

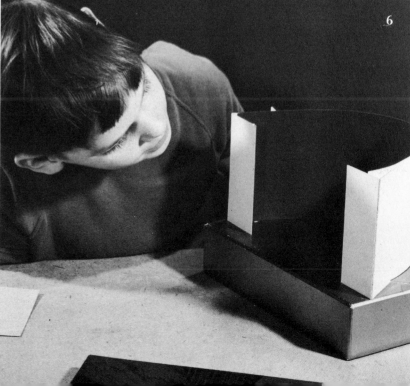

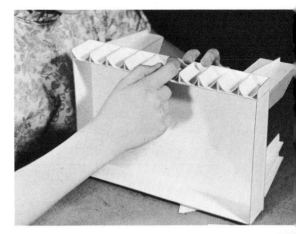

A MORE ELABORATE STAGE

Barbara-jo's stage is basically the same as Neil's. It has a top that fits on in the same way, and "keys" to hold circular backdrops. The parts that make it look more elaborate are all quite easy to make. The series of curves that run along the upper and lower borders of the stage, for example, are just little squares cut out from index cards squeezed between uprights of cardboard and glued in place. All sorts of fascinating lighting effects are made possible simply by cutting holes in the top. The "flats" that Barbara-jo places behind the throne are merely rectangles of poster board held together with sticky tape. The city scene was sketched on a length of colored construction paper with an ordinary felt-tip pen.

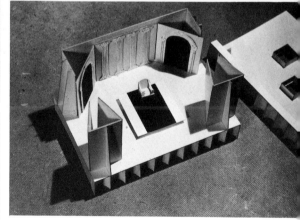

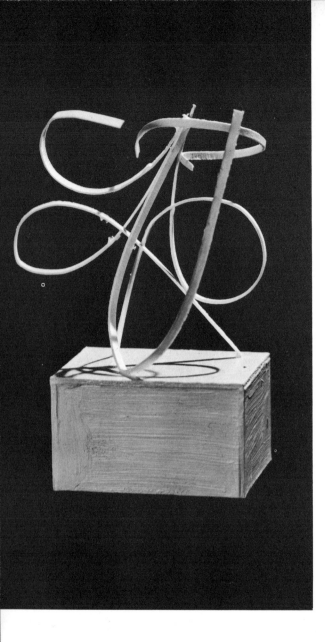

TINY SCULPTURE
YOU CAN HOLD
IN YOUR HAND

There is a thrill to building something really big in cardboard, but there is excitement too in constructing tiny, miniature things. All the examples here are made from scraps left over from other projects, and each piece of sculpture is extremely small. Knowing how each piece was made might give you some ideas for original miniatures of your own. The cowboy started out as a roll of very light cardboard, glued and flattened to give the head an oval look. A circle of flat cardboard was curved for the hat brim, and tiny strips of cardboard provided the features. The geometric-looking construction on the right is made from half-inch strips of stiff poster board. Each part is so light that the central upright can support them all with no trouble.

Very thin strips of Strathmore board wound around a pencil contribute the complicated curves of this free-form sculpture on its painted cardboard base.

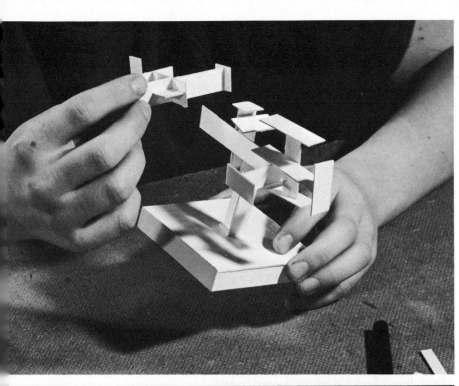

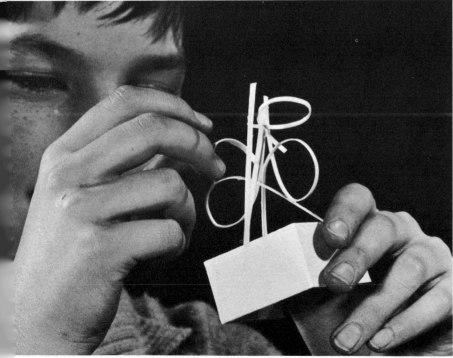

DESIGN AS YOU BUILD

What is it that you like most about your favorite building? Probably its over-all shape, and the way in which one part relates comfortably to the next. If a building is basically unattractive, no amount of fussing with decoration will save its appearance. What may start out as an attractive structure can also become an eyesore when there is too much ornamentation, or if inappropriate detail is added. David guarantees the success of his model by creating simple, well-designed basic shapes and limiting their decoration to a very few clean-cut details.

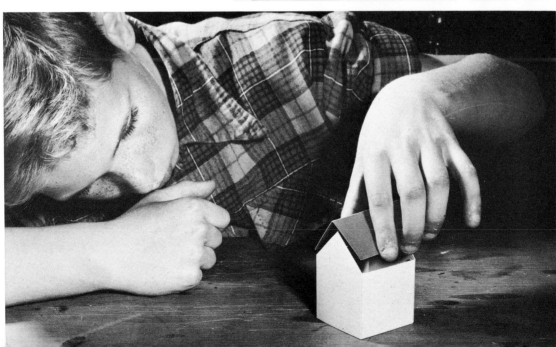

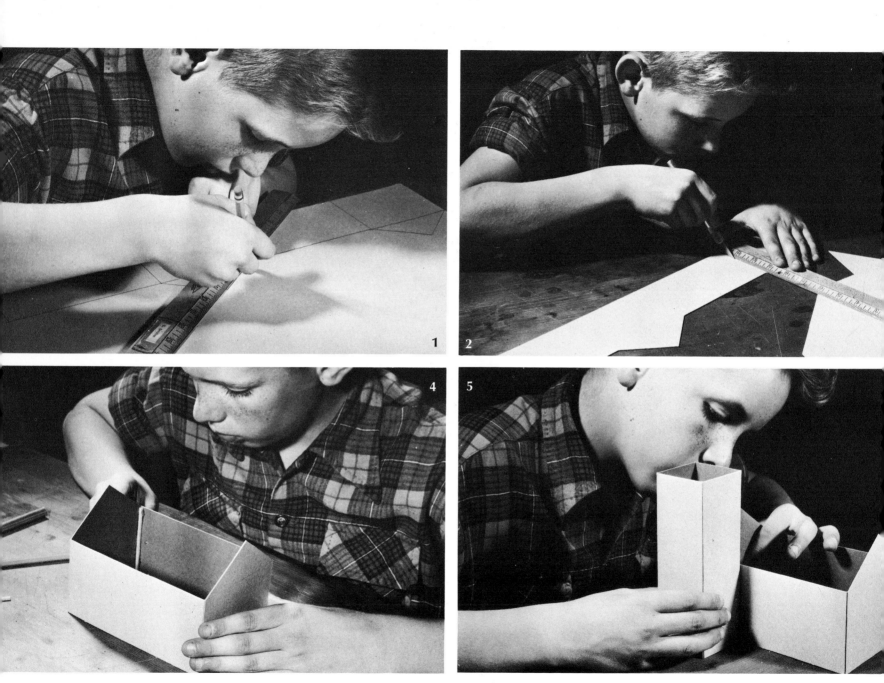

1. David decides to build a church with a tower. He begins by drawing a plan of the sides of the church on a sheet of white cardboard.

2. Then he uses an X-acto knife and a steel-edged ruler to cut out the sides in one continuous strip. He tries to slice right through the cardboard with each cut to ensure clean edges.

3. Just as he did with his trial model, David scores the cardboard wherever the corners fall and then folds the cardboard back on itself to keep the corner edges neat. He adds a strip of balsa wood where the ends meet so that he will be able to make a firm joint.

4. Bending the walls into position, he glues the ends in place. The balsa strips is set in the thickness of the cardboard so that the walls will be flush. He holds the structure steady until the glue dries.

5. The procedure used in making the main walls is repeated in constructing the tower which David glues to the church.

6. The model is strengthened by adding diagonal braces of scrap cardboard on the inside. Then David spreads glue along the bottom edges.

7. Now David places the model in a suitable position on a cardboard base and holds it until the glue is dry.

8. (Facing page) Squares of scrap cardboard are used to make the top of the tower. David tries several arrangements before he finds the one he likes.

9. Balsa stripping (1/8″ x 1/8″) and progressively smaller squares of cardboard combine in layers to complete the tower design.

10. He now plans the roof of the church. He scores a large rectangle of cardboard down the center, and then measures to find out where he must cut it so that it will fit around the tower.

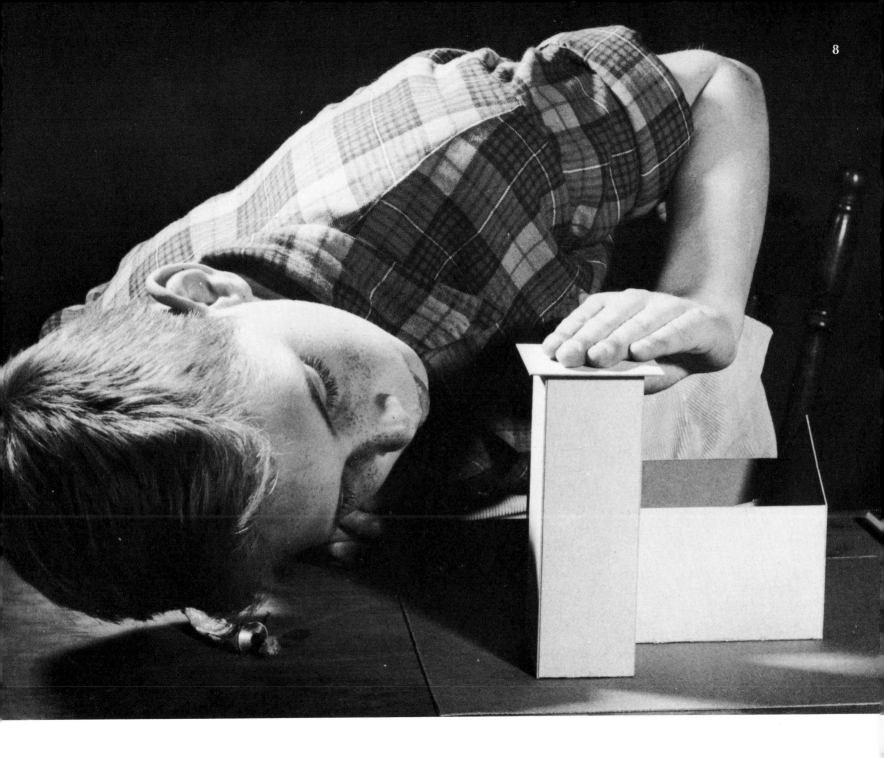

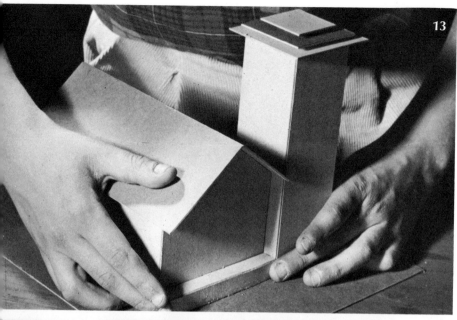

11. David uses a scrap of cardboard to measure the distance he must cut into the roof to make it fit snugly around the tower. He finds this method more accurate than measuring with a ruler.

12. The roof is creased and checked for snugness around the tower.

13. When the fit is satisfactory, it is glued into place. David chose a contrasting color of cardboard for this part of his model in preference to a painted roof.

14. He adds a long "planter" (later filled with scraps of sponge to represent plants) of scored and folded cardboard.

15. A study of the model from all sides convinces David that an addition is needed at one end. It is planned and built in the same manner as the rest of the model and is then glued to the base.

16. Balsa stripping (1/8″ x 1/8″) provides interesting detail and breaks up the plain surface.

SHADOW ART FROM CARDBOARD STRIPS

Some artists create with color, but others like to work only with light and shadow. Each project here is made from strips of shirt cardboard glued to a base of the same material. Although nothing else is used, the effect is as exciting and attention-getting as if an artist had worked with expensive art materials. Light and shadow have provided the magic touch that has transformed discarded shirt cardboard into something well worth more than a second glance. If you were looking at the real examples themselves, you would see that each time the light is shifted the designs take on a new appearance, and the expression on the cardboard face is changed. It is this lively shifting back and forth of light and shadow that intrigues some artists so much that they spend their whole lives working with these quicksilver qualities.

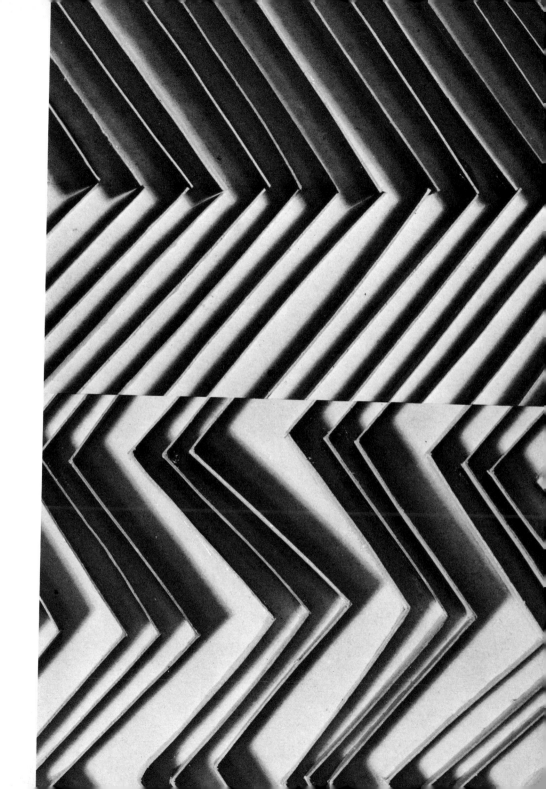

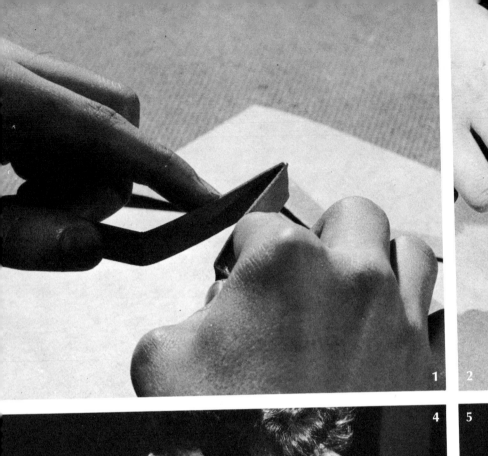

1

2

4

5

3

6

1. To make a face, Georgina scores a strip of shirt cardboard where she would like it to bend, then starts to manipulate it into the outline of a man's head.

2. She puts glue on the edges of the cardboard strips . . .

3. . . . and positions each part of the head on a cardboard base.

4. She glues on the hair . . .

5. . . . finishes an eye . . .

6. . . . adds a fancy collar, and her face is completed!

51

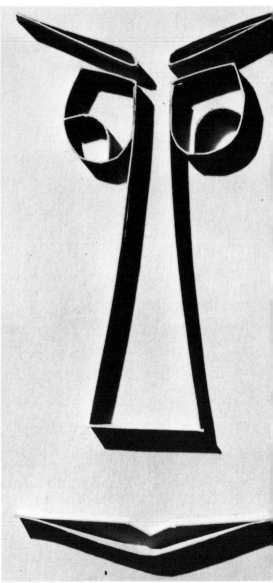

Colored gravel, the kind used in fish tanks, adds brilliance and texture to this imaginative sun. Although the lines and shadows of projects such as this are dramatic in themselves, poster paint, colored papers, and textured materials can suggest new and even more fascinating ways to work with cardboard strips.

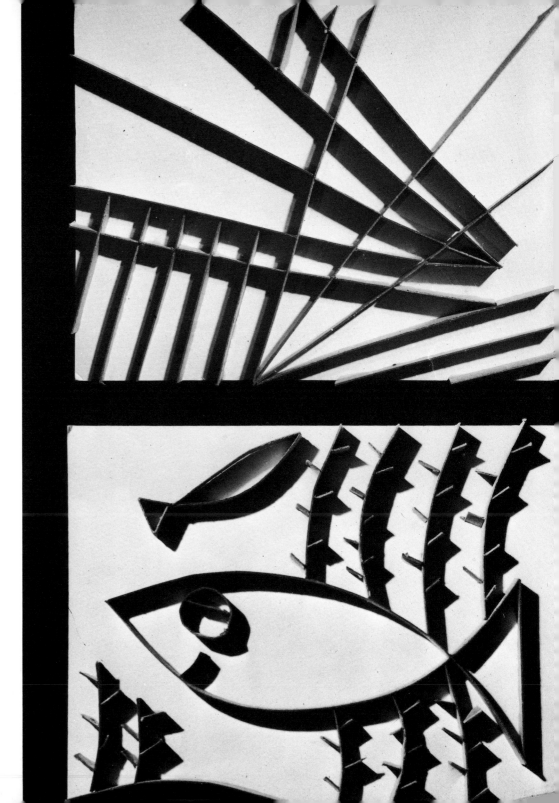

Each example on these two pages is very much different from the next, yet all were made by the same eleven-year-old. His work proves that you don't necessarily have to have expensive materials to be creative in art. Even the simplest materials provide unlimited opportunities for original work. In fact, the greatest challenge is to make something exciting and beautiful out of material that most people would discard as not having any value.

GLEN MAKES
A CARDBOARD MASK

Man, from earliest times, has made masks. Primitive man used them in his religious and tribal ceremonies. The Greeks and Japanese disguised their actors in masks. Today we all enjoy being scared and scaring other people with masks at Halloween. Masks are part of our art heritage. Masks can be decorative too, and Glen makes one here, not to wear, but to hang in his room as a decoration. Notice how, as in the cardboard-strip faces, shadows add character to Glen's mask, in this case giving it an ominous, mysterious look. Cardboard is a good material for mask-making, as it can be twisted and rolled into all sorts of shapes but is still stiff enough to hold whatever form the final design turns out to be.

Glen begins his mask by making the circular shapes he will use for the eyes and mouth. He cuts a strip of shirt cardboard, loosens the fibers by pulling it back and forth over the edge of a table, rolls it into the shape he wants, and staples the ends together.

1. Glen places the eye shapes where he feels they will look best.

2. Then he positions the mouth.

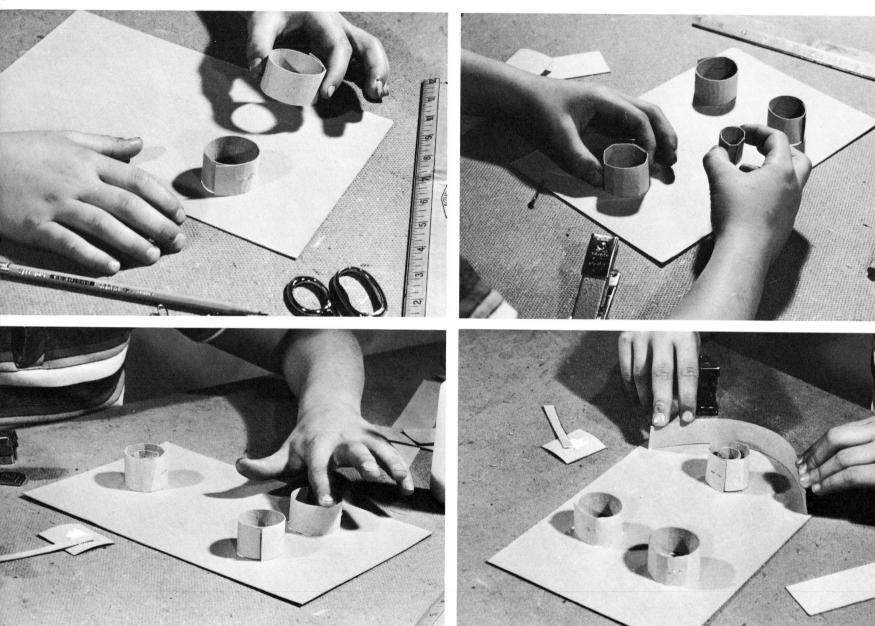

5. He glues the eyes to the shirt cardboard base.

6. A chin is added . . .

58

3. He puts some quick-drying glue on a square of cardboard . . .

4. . . . and applies it with a length of scrap cardboard to the edge of the eye shapes.

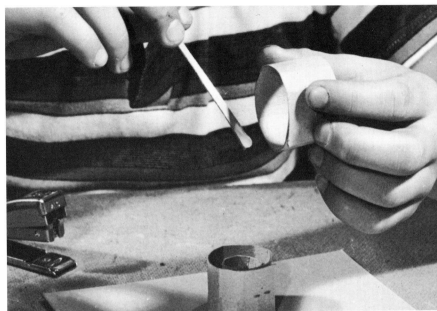

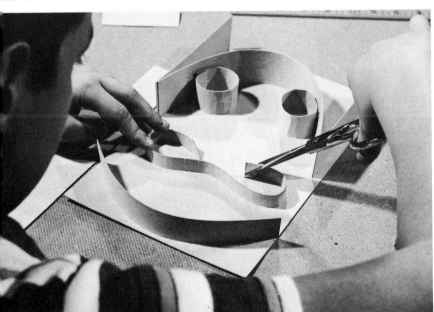

7. . . . and a mustache is glued on and trimmed.

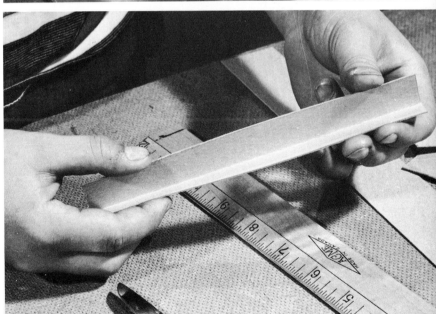

8. A wide strip of cardboard is scored and creased down the center to make a nose.

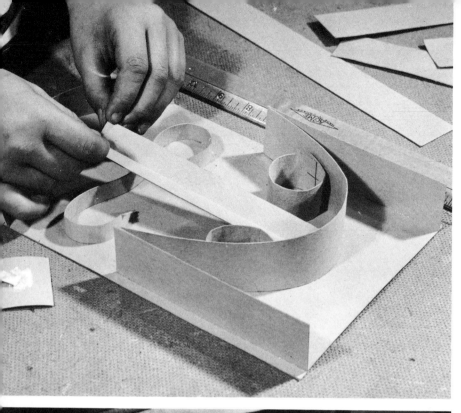

9. The nose is glued in place. Notice how Glen has it rest on the mustache so that it is raised and, therefore, looks more three-dimensional.

10. All the while Glen has been busy gluing the parts of his face together, he has been planning in his mind just where to place things so that they would look best. Although he has made two rings for the mouth instead of one, as in both eyes, he wasn't sure it would look just right, so he didn't glue them down. Now he has decided to keep them, and so they are glued into place. If you make a mask, your mind will have to be constantly alert in order to make wise decisions on just what to do next as you put your mask together.

11. Glen has made up triangular units to represent hair. He tries different ways of arranging them.

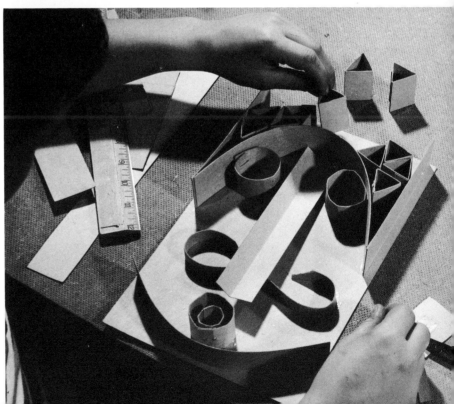

12. As soon as he finds an arrangement he likes, he glues the hair in place and his mask is finished.

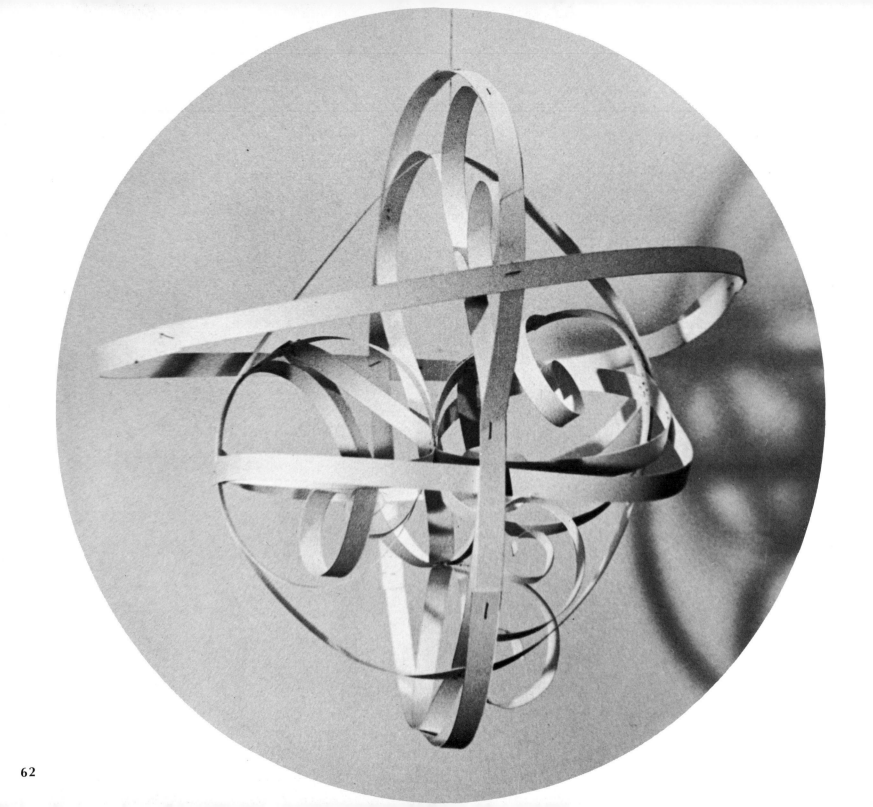

SPACE DESIGNS

Slowly turning in the air, casting constantly changing shadows, space designs are so fascinating that it is hard to keep your eyes off them. They are also fascinating to build, because in no time at all the tiniest pile of cardboard strips can be transformed into a giant design. All you need to make a space design is a stapler or some sticky tape and long strips of light cardboard. And the process is so unmessy that you can build your design right on the living-room carpet and no one will complain!

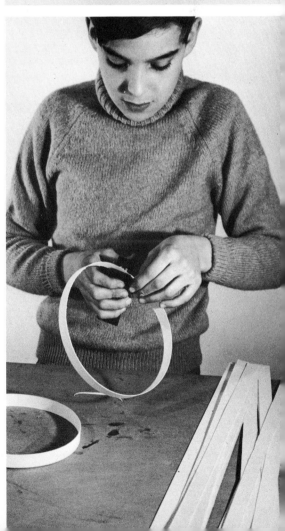

Peter begins his space design by cutting thin cardboard (in this case, Strathmore board) into long strips and, first, stapling the ends of the strips together to make circles and, finally, stapling the circles together to make shapes.

Peter adds more and more strips and his design grows and grows. While the technique is simple, he has to keep thinking where he should put the next strip. Should he use another ring or just add a curving length of cardboard? Would more strips here make his design unbalanced? He keeps holding the design up and turning it around in order to come up with the answers to these questions.

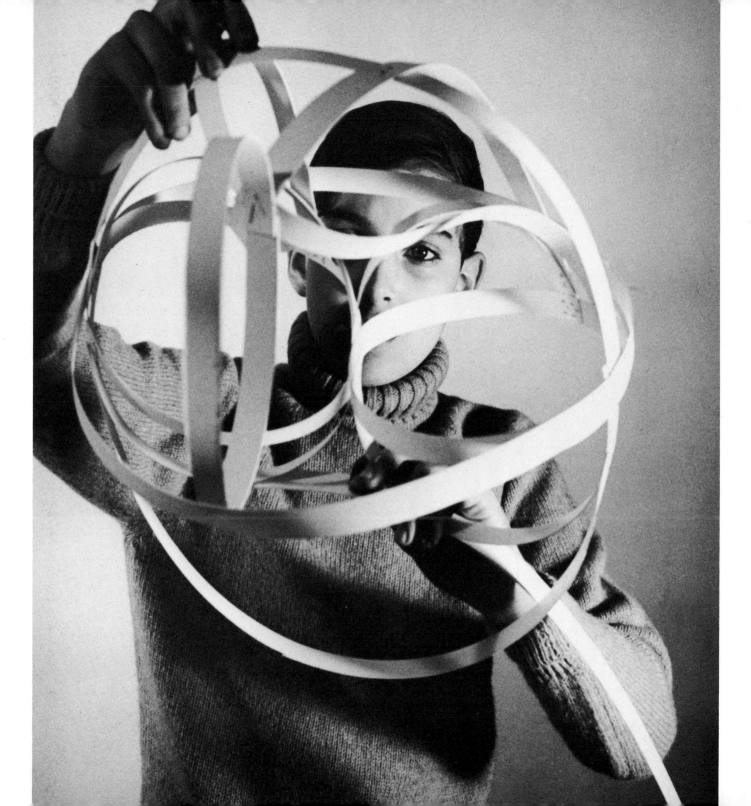

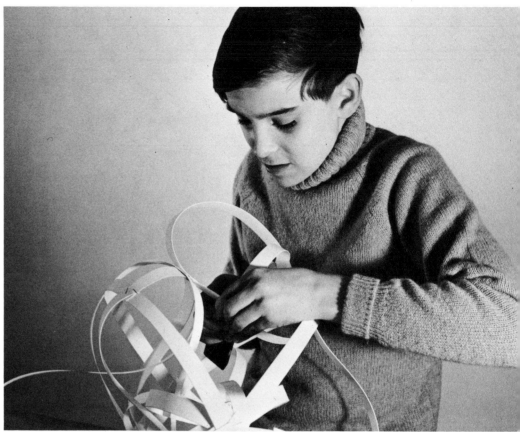

When the main structure of his design is complete, Peter wraps cardboard strips around his fingers to make curls which he will use to fill in the empty spaces left in his space composition. Finally, his space design is complete and he hangs it up at a point of balance so that it can revolve freely and be seen to advantage.

A BOX ON A BOX ON A BOX ON A BOX MAKES A TOWER

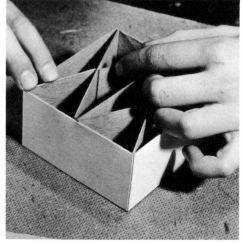

Cardboard boxes come in all shapes and sizes and are designed to hold a thousand and one different things. But what could be more interesting to put in a box than a design? Even if you work only with square boxes that are exactly the same size you will be surprised at the number of different designs that will fit snugly into them. In fact, there seems no end to the ways in which you can design the inside of a box. Fortunately, this is just as well, as completing one box design is almost certain to intrigue you into trying another . . . and another! Before you know it you will have quite a number of designs on hand. Then, if you like, you can show off your work to advantage by arranging your designs so they create a handsome geometric sculpture. The boxes can be glued to one another, or left free in case you want to rearrange your composition from time to time to create new forms.

The box designs here are open at both ends so that the light shining through each one influences its appearance. The same designs painted and set against colored cardboard backgrounds, a white design backed by blue, an orange and black against yellow for example would, of course, look quite different. Colored backgrounds of cellophane instead of cardboard allow pink or blue or amber light to flood the interior of each box and tint the surface of each design with color to create still another effect. Because each box is, in a way, like a little stage, it provides a dramatic setting for whatever design you care to build within it.

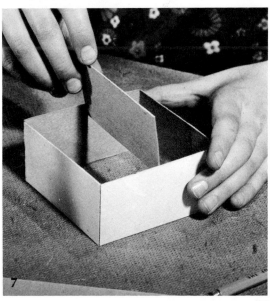

1. Barbara-jo begins her box design by dividing a strip of shirt cardboard into four equal parts.

2. She scores the cardboard where it will fall . . .

3. . . . creases each score . . .

4. . . . and glues the ends together.

5. She measures off the distance of a crosspiece she will use in her design, not with a ruler but by eye . . .

6. . . . cuts it to size . . .

7. . . . and tests to see if it will fit.

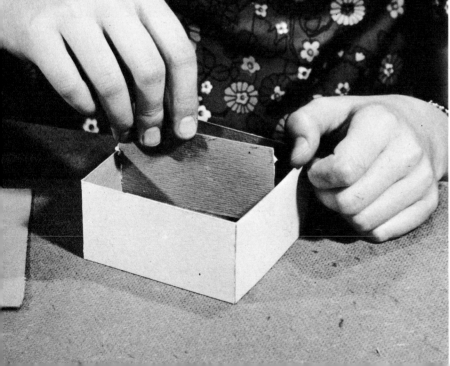

8. She squeezes some quick-drying glue on to a square of cardboard . . .

9. . . . dips the ends of her crosspiece into it . . .

10. . . . and slides it into position.

11. Now she uses a ruler to make sure the first piece is at the center line of the box. The glue will stay moist long enough for her to make any adjustments that are needed.

12. Barbara-jo adds new pieces to her design. First, measuring by eye, then slipping each new piece into position without gluing to see how it will look.

13. After deciding on the design, she glues the pieces in place.

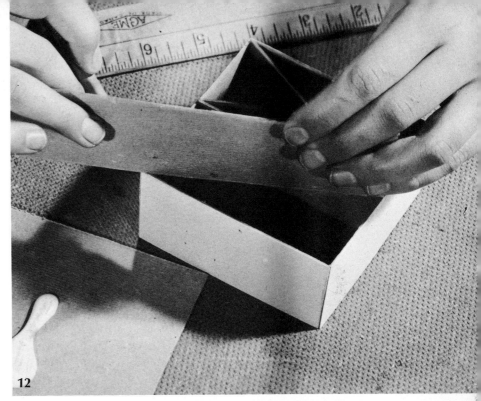

12

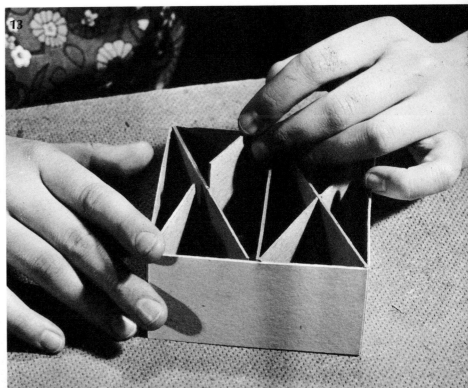

13

14. After she has completed several box designs, Barbara-jo decides to build a tower. She spreads glue on top of one box . . .

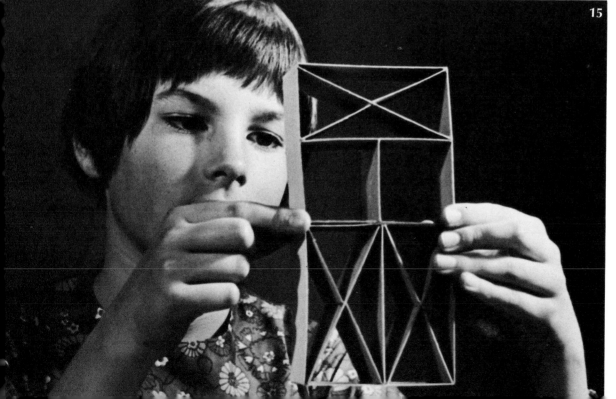

15. . . . and places another on top.

16. She glues two more units together in the same way . . .

17. . . . securing them with paper clips, which she can remove when the glue is dry.

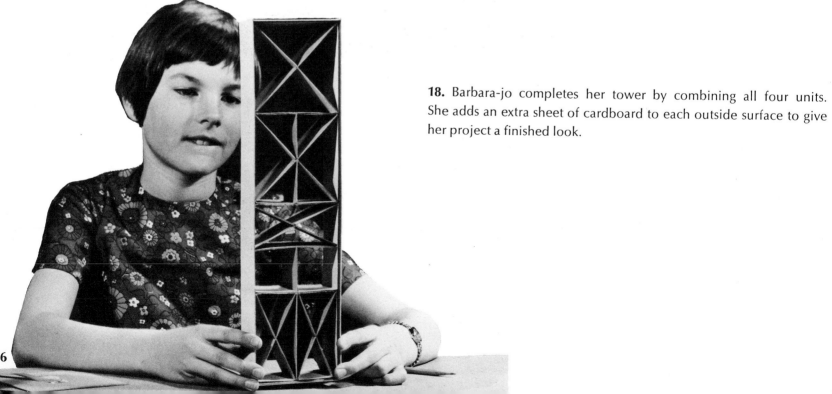

18. Barbara-jo completes her tower by combining all four units. She adds an extra sheet of cardboard to each outside surface to give her project a finished look.

The appearance of Barbara-jo's tower changes as the light changes. It looks particularly handsome when the light shines through its design spaces. Each square creates its own shadow patterns which, shifting with the light, bring life and excitement to her design.

To most people a discarded shirt cardboard would not suggest a starting point for creative activity. They would definitely not imagine it as the origin of a striking piece of sculpture. Yet when you know how to build with cardboard, just such a piece of scrap material seems like treasure trove!

REAL SCULPTURE
YOU CAN BUILD AT HOME

Fascinating sculpture can be made from the simplest of cardboard shapes. Here Gary cuts up a discarded shirt cardboard into a number of triangular shapes, and glues them together to create a many-sided, three-dimensional composition. Although he arranges the shapes first one way then another until he finds the composition he likes, all his attempts have pleasing possibilities because, as the pieces are triangular, they relate well to one another.

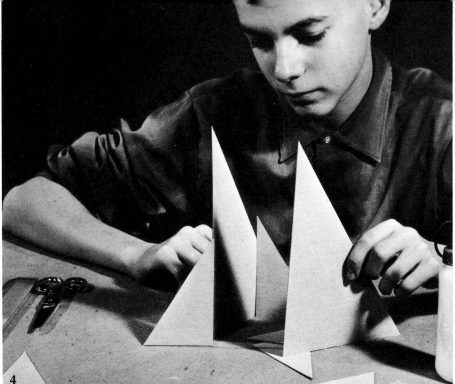

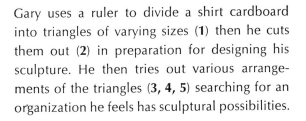

Gary uses a ruler to divide a shirt cardboard into triangles of varying sizes (1) then he cuts them out (2) in preparation for designing his sculpture. He then tries out various arrangements of the triangles (3, 4, 5) searching for an organization he feels has sculptural possibilities.

6. Gary covers the edge of a triangle with glue.

7. He positions it at right angles against the main upright piece to act as a brace which helps his sculpture to stand straight.

8. If a section is extended, Gary supports it with anything that is at hand. In this case he uses an eraser to keep the extended section from dropping out of position.

9. As more and more pieces are added, the sculpture becomes more complex and Gary has to be cautious that his design will not become confusing.

10. Finally, the last piece is added and Gary's sculpture is complete.

9

Gary's second piece of sculpture is made up of rectangles instead of triangles. Because of this, the lively spiky quality of his first design is replaced by the architectural massiveness of this one. Every time you change the basic element in sculpture you change the feeling of the finished piece.

CORRUGATED
CARDBOARD DESIGN

Most cardboard designs are three-dimensional, made by gluing pieces of cardboard together. While two-dimensional corrugated cardboard design seems much simpler, you will still need your wits about you to meet the challenge of making something worthwhile out of nothing more than a single piece of cardboard.

Each kind of cardboard suggests a special way of working. Double-faced corrugated cardboard has a layer of rippled cardboard sandwiched between two layers of sturdy cover paper. Many cardboard boxes are made from double-faced corrugated cardboard.

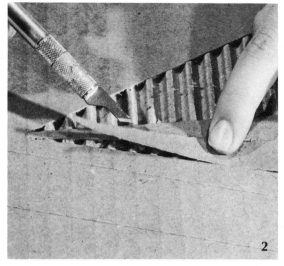

1. Barbara-jo begins her corrugated cardboard design by cutting through the first layer of cardboard with an X-acto knife.

2. She used the point of the knife to lift up a flap of cardboard . . .

3. . . . then peels it back to reveal the corrugations underneath, using the tip of the X-acto blade to help free any parts that do not peel easily.

4. She rests one hand on the cardboard to keep it from pulling up as she peels off its top layer.

Cutting through the top layer of this kind of cardboard to expose the ripples underneath is a technique which will suggest all sorts of design ideas to you. As Barbara-jo demonstrates here, you cut along the outline of a design shape and then peel the cover paper off so that the texture of the corrugations stands out against the contrasting smoothness of the surrounding cardboard.

Some pieces of cardboard peel without any difficulty. Others, perhaps more securely glued, can give trouble. Very often, one side of a sheet of double-faced cardboard will be better for your purposes than the other. Before beginning a project with corrugated cardboard it is best to experiment to find just the right piece and the right side for the design you have in mind.

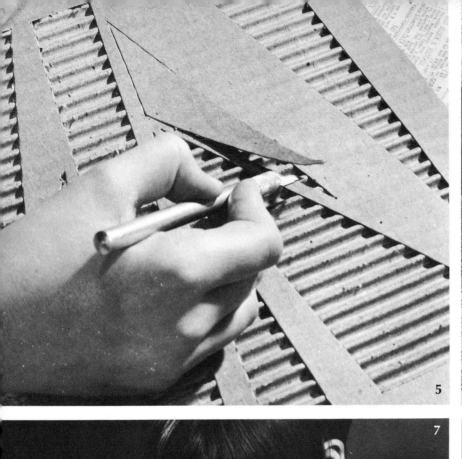

5. Barbara-jo has been careful to leave sufficient space between the parts of her design so that the dividing background strips will not pull up.

6. She carefully peels off the last bit of the top layer.

7. Using the dull side of her X-acto blade she scratches off any bits of glue or paper that still remain stuck to the corrugations.

8. Here is Barbara-jo's finished design, boldly defined by the rich texture of its corrugations.

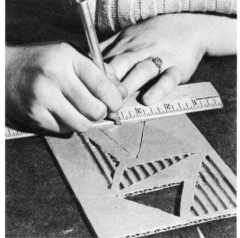

Wendy makes a corrugated design in the same way Barbara-jo did, but cuts right through in some cases so that she can remove whole areas of cardboard. When she mounts her design on a piece of colored cardboard the color will show through the openings to give her design a different look.

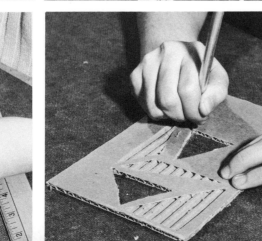

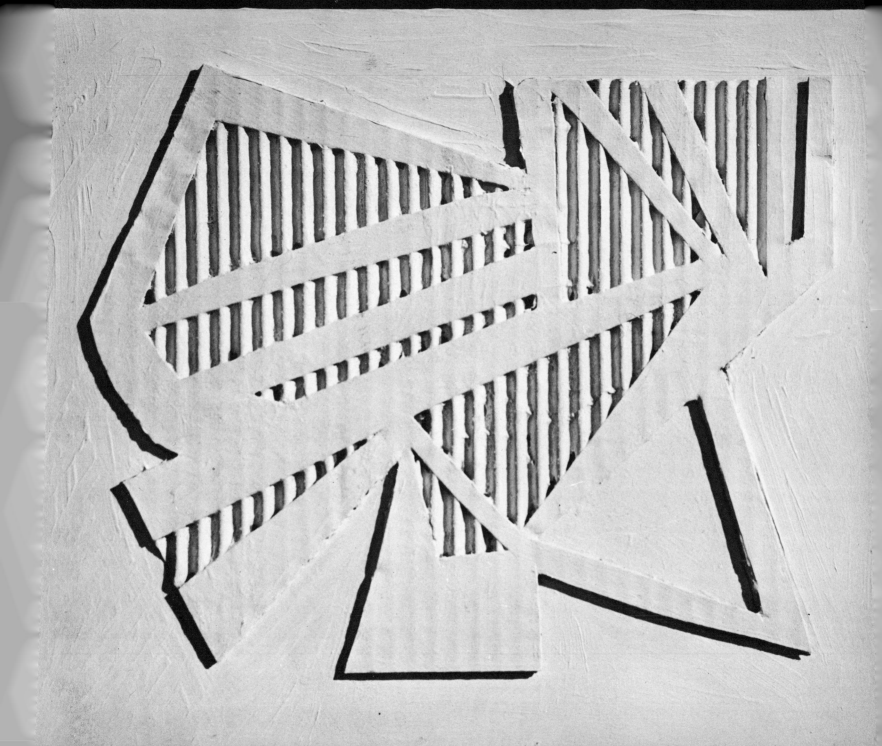

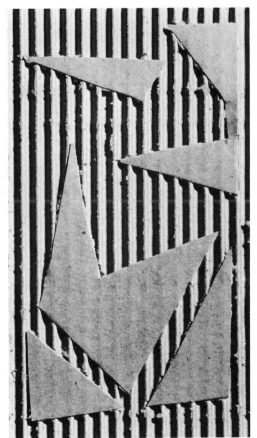

Corrugated design can be varied in many ways. On page 86, for example, we see how a coat of poster paint can make a corrugated design look like a plaster carving. Here, on page 87, a simple pencil line adds enrichment too, but in quite a different way. Pieces of corrugation cut out and glued back at contrasting angles create yet another effect. In a fourth composition, Barbara-jo's procedure is reversed so that the cover paper, instead of the corrugations, indicates each design shape.

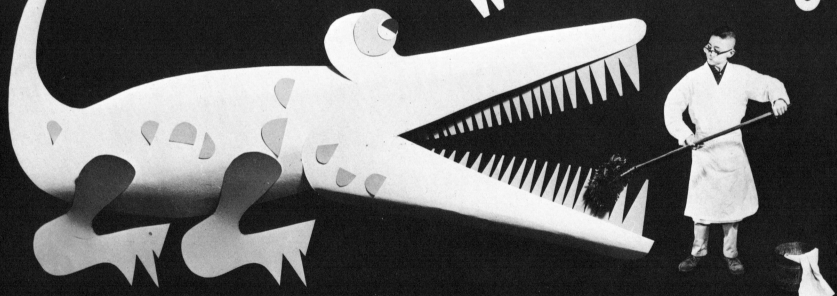

POSTER-MAKING WITH SCULPTURED CARDBOARD

To be effective a poster must have attention value. It must be inventive, eye-catching, imaginative. Kennie's posters have these qualities because the sculptured cardboard crocodile stands out boldly from the background to add an unexpected dimension to the design.

A piece of sculpture, such as Kennie's crocodile, that is modeled but only enough to give it partial three-dimensionality, is called "relief" sculpture. While the "relief" technique is shown here in a poster series, both abstract designs and realistic themes are effective when they are expressed in cardboard "relief."

After he had modeled his crocodile in light cardboard, Kennie had his sister take his picture in the poses you see above. Then he cut

the figure away from the background and placed it in an appropriate position on the poster for which it was intended. Although it is fun to use original photos, first-rate posters can be produced by illustrations cut from magazines.

Kennie's posters are "photo posters," which he made by using his crocodile over and over again combined with new arrangements of photographs and letters. He then had his finished posters photographed so that he could have multiple copies. While having photo copies made is a handy technique if posters are needed in quantity, a cardboard sculpture poster is always most attention-getting in its original form because the viewer can see its actual three-dimensional "relief" effect.

1. Kennie cuts out a crocodile shape from a sheet of light cardboard. Before he started his cardboard figure he experimented with newspaper in order to work out his idea.

2. He cuts out the body shape first.

3. Then he matches teeth and legs of colored construction paper with the white cardboard of the body.

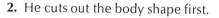
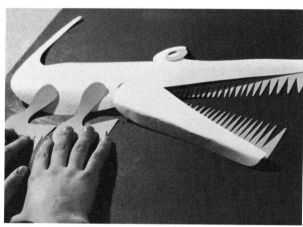
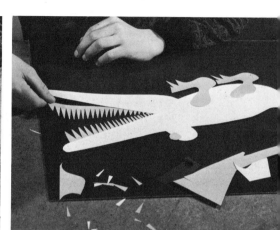

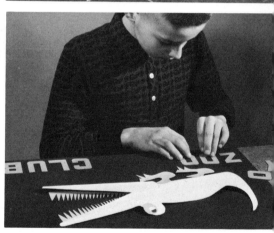

5. He tries the flat legs against the roundness of the body.

6. Notice how much more realistic the crocodile looks now that it has been "sculptured."

7. Kennie uses commercial letters but he could just as well have hand-lettered his poster or cut out letters from magazines.

4. Now that he can visualize the finished crocodile, Kennie "rolls" and creases the edges of the body to create a three-dimensional effect.

8. Smaller letters spell out the message to complete the first phase of his poster-making.

YOU CAN BUILD

Once you get the feel of working with cardboard you can build anything you want with it. You won't need plans or instructions or help. Plastic kits which allow you to build only one thing won't seem nearly as much fun as they used to ·be. There were no plans for any of the projects pictured here. Each one was invented by its maker. Cardboard tubes and cores suggested the man on the left.

ANYTHING YOU WANT

The tugboat didn't present too many problems as the cardboard from which it was made did not have to be creased or twisted into unusual shapes. The imaginative design for a ski lodge on the right, relying only on straight lines and flat surfaces for its effectiveness, demonstrates how the simplest of approaches to building with cardboard can often be the most successful.

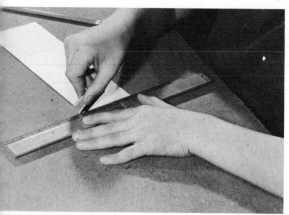

EASY-TO-MAKE CUBES BECOME AN IMPRESSIVE BUILDING

Neil demonstrates how to make a simple cube grow from a strip of cardboard (1, 2, 3). The building he is holding (4) is much larger but it is built in exactly the same way. Its base (5) is much more complex but it too has the same boxlike structure. While strips of cardboard have been added to give detail and tiny figures used to make it look larger by contrast, we can see that this model of an important-looking building is still only a series of cubes.

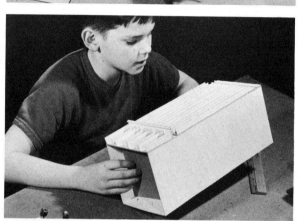

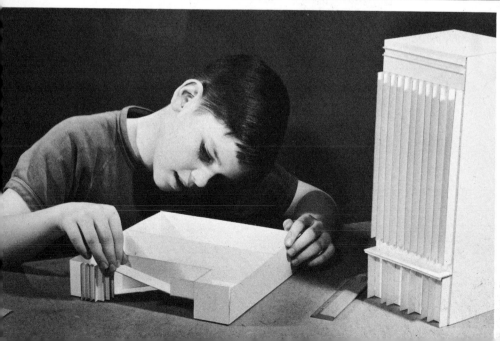

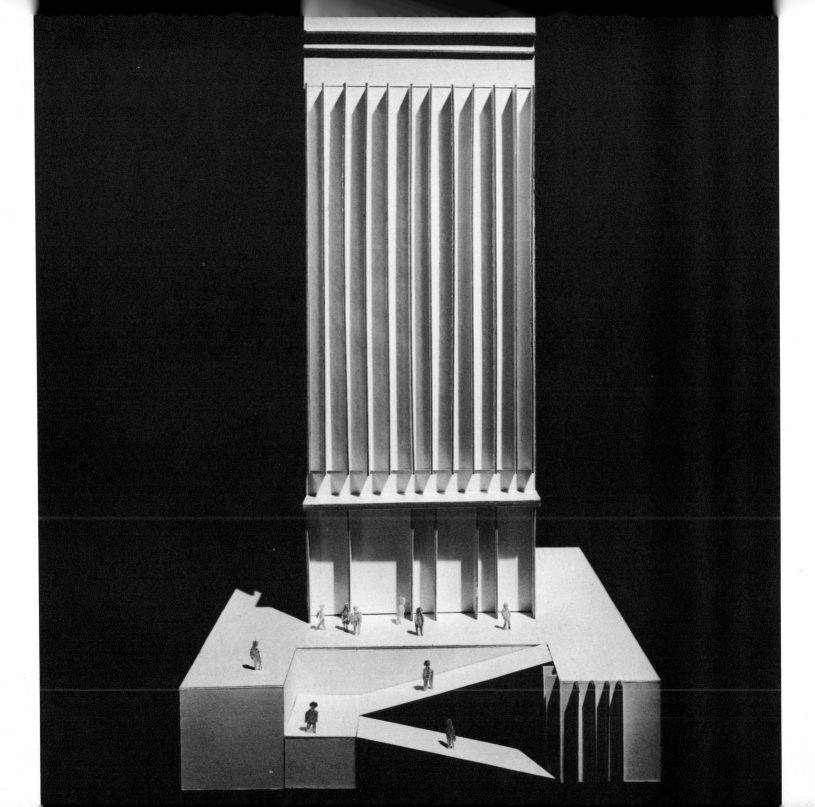

ACKNOWLEDGMENTS

Appreciation is extended to the editors of **Arts and Activities, The Grade Teacher,** and **School Arts** for their cooperation and help.

Special acknowledgment is due Steve Barrell, Ken Campbell, Mark Davis, Gary Harmel, David Hutton, Peter Kelley, Wendy Lockhart, Glen MacLean, Van MacLean, Neil MacRae, Barbara-jo McIntosh, Karen McQueen and Georgina Price, whose creativity and willingness to work before the camera made possible the many photographs which illustrate the book.

Book design by John Lidstone and George H. Buehler.